OBJECT LESSONS FROM THE BIBLE

Wesley T. Runk

BAKER BOOK HOUSE
Grand Rapids, Michigan 49506

PHOTOLITHOPRINTED BY CUSHING - MALLOY, INC.
ANN ARBOR, MICHIGAN, UNITED STATES OF AMERICA

TABLE OF CONTENTS

ARE YOU A BUILDING BLOCK?

Romans 12:1-5, vs. 3: For by the grace given to me I bid every one among you not to think of himself more highly than he ought to think, but to think with sober judgment.

Object: Some building blocks.

Good morning, boys and girls. Today we are going to talk about you and the way that you think. Everyone likes to think about himself, and today we are going to give you a chance to do just that. What do you think about you? If someone asked you to describe yourself what would you tell him? I'll give you some hints. Are you good-looking, strong, beautiful, smart, funny, happy, wide awake? Are these the things that people see in you when they talk about you, or are you ugly, weak, dumb, sad, sleepy, rough? How do people think about you? I am going to ask a couple of people to tell me what they think about themselves. [*Choose a few children and let them talk for a couple of minutes.*]

Now let me show you something else. Have you ever taken blocks like this and stacked them on top of one another as high as you could? Have you? What happens when you get the stack too high? They fall. They fall all over the place so that there is nothing left but a couple of blocks on top of each other and the rest are spread out everywhere. It doesn't matter how neatly you stack them or how much time you spend on each of them, the same thing eventually happens — they fall and they fall hard.

The reason that we can talk about blocks and people in the same story is that these kinds of blocks and people are a lot alike. Some people think of themselves too highly. When they do they are just getting themselves in big trouble. Another way of saying it is that they are getting ready for a big fall. St. Paul tells us in his letter to the Romans that a man or woman should not think of himself or herself too highly or they are bound to have a bad fall. That means that you should not be conceited or brag too much. When you do, you are not only asking for trouble from other people, but you are also very displeasing to God. It is better not to think so much of yourself, but think instead of what you can do for others and for God. When we think too much of ourselves we are like the blocks that build themselves up too high. The next time may be the last time that you can say what you want to about yourself without taking a big fall. You never know which block is the highest until you put the last one on and then comes the big fall. So, instead of thinking how great you are and how wonderful others think you are, think about God and his power.

THE UNWRAPPED GIFTS

Romans 12:6-16a, vs. 6a: Having gifts that differ according to the grace given to us, let us use them . . .

Object: Some gifts that have never been unwrapped. They are things which people save rather than use.

Good morning, boys and girls. How many of you received a gift that you really liked last Christmas? Do you remember the gift that you liked the most? [*Let them answer.*] How many of you have some gifts that you have not opened yet? [*Wait for an answer.*] I wonder what it would be like to keep our gifts wrapped and open them just once in a while rather than opening them all on Christmas? How many would do that if I asked you to do it? I know some people who keep their gifts wrapped for years and never use them. Can you imagine receiving a gift and just putting it away in a drawer? I can't imagine doing it either, but I know some who do exactly that sort of thing.

Let me show you some of the things that I have found put away, and never used. [*Take out some packages of sheets and pillow cases, a shirt, a billfold and anything else that comes wrapped that can be shown.*] What would you think if you gave someone a gift like one of these and found it months or years later wrapped the same way it was when you gave it? [*Let them answer.*] I know how I would feel. I would think that the people didn't like the gift I gave them, or that they didn't need it, or they had so many gifts that they couldn't use my gift. That's the way all of us would feel.

The reason I have told you this is because God is the giver of magnificent gifts and many of the things that he gives to us are never used. I wonder how God feels about the person who is given a beautiful voice and never sings, or a great mind and never uses it for anything that helps others. Some people are given great gifts of healing and teaching, and when they are not used or shared it is like the person who takes the gifts that I have shown you and puts them away in a closet or drawer. God gives the gift so that it can be used and not saved. What good is a voice not used, or an idea that is not shared? It is like a sheet or pillowcase kept in a drawer or a billfold that is never opened. God gives gifts so that we will use them, and the wonderful thing about the gift is that as it is used and shared, God gives so much more. Now you must think about the talent or gift that God has given you and how you can use it. Just think how much fun it will be to share with others what you have, and know that there will always be a lot more given when you use what you have been given.

ROUGH SANDPAPER

Romans 12:16b to 21, vs. 21: Do not be overcome by evil, but overcome evil with good.

Object: A piece of wood that is easily scarred like pine and some sandpaper.

Good morning, boys and girls. Today we are going to have an experiment to show you how a piece of wood can be like a person. I just love a smooth piece of wood that has been freshly cut. It smells good, and it feels good. A piece of wood like this is just like a baby. When it is this fresh it is without any scars on the outside, but as it gets older and is used more and more, you begin to see marks here and there. [*Take a pencil and make some lines on the board.*] A board gets more than marks because sometimes it gets bumped and scratched and dented. [*Bump it against another board, scratch it with a nail.*] Now the real problems are starting to show up, and if something isn't done with it pretty soon it will be replaced by another board and thrown away. But there is something that can be done for the board that will bring it back fresh again so that it looks like new. Does anyone have any ideas about how we can fix up the board? [*Let them answer.*]

We could paint it, but another way that is used and should be used even before we paint it is to sand it with sandpaper. Look what happens to the marks and the scratches when we sand it. Do you see them disappearing? We are making good out of something that looked bad. People can do the same thing with their lives as we did with the board. A lot of people have things happen to them that we call sins. This kind of reminds us of bumps, dents, scratches and marks. At first they don't seem too bad, but as the time goes along we find that the sins are really making us look awful. We find that just saying that we are sorry or that we made a mistake is not enough. The Bible teaches us that we need to be forgiven for our sins by God and that we need to do something that will prevent us from doing bad things. It is when we start doing good things for people that we are like sandpaper. We can't do two things at once. When we are doing good, we cannot do bad. We need to overcome our sins by doing good for others. Sandpaper overcomes marks and scratches and love overcomes sin. So the next time you want to do something, make sure it is something good for someone else, and while you are doing it you will know that you are not only making someone happy, but you are keeping yourself from doing something wrong. Overcome evil with good.

HOW TO LOVE YOUR NEIGHBOR

Romans 13:8-10, vs. 9b: "You shall love your neighbor as yourself . . ."

Object: A mirror and your own arms.

Good morning, boys and girls. Today we are going to talk about love and what it really means. The Bible teaches us that we should love ourselves and also our neighbors. What does it mean to love? I know what a lot of people call love, and I don't think that it is really love. Some people think that love is saying nice things or holding someone in a very fond way. The Bible teaches us that we should love our neighbors as we love ourselves. Now can you imagine what this might look like if love was only saying nice things or holding people in a certain way? Let me show you what I mean.

Suppose we are talking about the holding part. [*Turn your back to the children, and place your own arms about you in such a way that it appears that you are being embraced.*] "I think I am wonderful and I feel so good to myself that I hardly know what to do." How does that look? Kind of sick? How about this one: [*Hold up the mirror.*] "I am the most handsome person in the world and I love me dearly." That is really bad, and I am sure that you agree with me that this is not what the Bible means when it says that we should love our neighbors as we love ourselves. Then what does it mean?

Love is sharing with others as you care for yourself. You love yourself by the way that you care for yourself. When you are thirsty you get yourself some water. When a neighbor is thirsty you give him a drink. When he is hungry you feed him and when he needs a place to stay you let him stay with you. Those are the kinds of things that you do for yourself when you can do them. You visit people when they are lonely and help them when they are sick. These are the kinds of ways in which you show a neighbor that you love him. Sometimes you will find friends and strangers in need of the things that you do for yourself, and that is when God tells us that we should show our love for them just as we love ourselves. We must always think well of others and speak well of them, but when we have the chance to do good we should also remember to do it.

Love is more than saying nice things or holding people in special ways. We should learn this early so that we don't miss our opportunities to be as God wants us to be.

YOU'RE BEAUTIFUL TO GOD!

Colossians 3:12-17, vs. 14: And above all these put on love, which binds everything together in perfect harmony.

Object: Some pieces of paper and a paperback book.

Good morning, boys and girls. It is certainly nice to see you all together. There is something about being together that is good, and is different from everything else. I wonder what it is that brings us together? Do you know? [*Let them answer.*] Those are pretty good answers, but let us look around for the right answer.

I have brought with me today something that will show you what it is that brings us together. [*Hold up the pieces of paper.*] Now here are some pieces of paper that are good for writing on or coloring on. Each piece of paper is like a person, just like you. They are all individuals, and if I drop them from my hand they all go their own way. There is nothing to hold them together. There are some people like that, and there is something very sad about them, for there is nothing to hold them together.

Now I have some more paper, [*Hold up book*] only this time the paper is held together. What do we call paper when it is like this? That's right, it is a book. What holds a book together? What holds this book together? Glue, that's right. We call this "binding." The book is bound and held together. Now we can't glue people so that they will stay together, but we have something that works even better. It is the same thing that brings you here this morning. It is called love. God's love is the same as glue to books. It brings it all together and we enjoy it.

That is what is so wonderful about being a Christian. We have God's love and it makes all of us beautiful. We are beautiful to God and to one another and we love to be with each other. St. Paul learned this from God a long time ago, and he wrote it down so that we would all know what it is that holds us together. I hope that you can feel the love of God today as I can. I hope that it will keep us together for as long as we live, just as the glue binds pages together and makes them into a book.

JESUS ONLY!

2 Peter 1:16-21, vs. 19: And we have the prophetic word made more sure. You will do well to pay attention to this as to a lamp shining in a dark place, until the day dawns and the morning star rises in your hearts.

Object: A piece of posterboard with one black dot.

Good morning, boys and girls. Have you ever noticed how some things get your attention quickly and you never forget them? I have something here with me this morning that is like that to most people. I want to show it to you, but you have to promise me that you will tell me what it means as soon as you see it. Do you promise? That's good. Everyone get ready. [*Take the poster board with the black dot in one corner and show it to them.*] Tell me what you see. [*Let them answer.*]

A black dot. Is there anything else? Do you see anything else but the black dot? Nothing? I am surprised that you don't see this beautiful white poster board. The only thing that you see is the dot and it is so small compared to the whole poster board. But that is what I wanted you to say, and I am glad that you noticed the dot because it helps my story a lot.

Some things stick out so much that we cannot miss them. Jesus was like that, especially at certain times. Today we want to talk about one of those times. Jesus was transfigured, which is a big word meaning that Jesus was made as bright as the shining sun. Some of the disciples saw him like this and they were amazed. There they were talking to Jesus when all of a sudden he became bright, so bright that they had to hide their eyes. They also heard a voice from heaven telling them that Jesus was God's Son and that God was very pleased with Jesus. When things like that happen you notice it, and you don't notice anything else. Jesus made people certain of what they believed. When

Jesus is around you and teaching you he is like that dot on the paper. There is nothing else that is noticed except Jesus.

It is the Transfiguration and things like it that make people certain of what they believe about Jesus. You can go home today and make a dot like this on a piece of plain white paper and it will help you to remind yourself of how Jesus stands out above everything else and helps us believe in him. Jesus makes us certain of God and his love for us.

YOU WEAR A LEASH, TOO

1 Corinthians 9:24-10:5, vs. 25: Every athlete exercises self-control in all things. They do it to receive a perishable wreath, but we an imperishable.

Object: A dog leash.

Good morning, boys and girls, I want to ask you how you got here this morning. [*Let them answer.*] Did someone bring you in the car? Did you have to do any walking? Did you run this morning when you should not have run, or did anybody tell you to walk when you were running? [*Let them answer.*] Sometimes it is pretty hard to just walk when we want to run and our mothers and fathers tell us to stop running or to sit down on a chair and be quiet. We get out of control. Have you ever been told to sit down and be quiet? [*Let them answer.*] I know what that is like, because my mother and father used to have to tell me to do those things. I suppose that I did what they told me, although it was pretty hard sometimes.

We have another way of making some of our friends walk or stay with us when we want them to. How many of you have a dog? Dogs are great friends, aren't they? Do you ever take your dog for a walk and put the leash on him? A leash helps you control the dog so that he will not run in the street or get away from you when you are walking. In some places like big cities you have to keep your dog on a leash so that you have control of the dog at all times. Do you think that would work pretty well on boys and girls? We could buy a collar for every boy and girl and then get a leash and keep control in that way. How do you think that would work? [*Let them answer.*] I don't think that you would like that very much.

People are supposed to have self-control. One of the reasons that your parents tell you about all of your mistakes is so that you can learn self-control. That means you can take care of yourself and you don't need a leash.

Christians are taught the greatest self-control because Christians do not need the law. Christians do more than the law. The law teaches you not to hurt anyone, but that is all. A leash keeps a dog from biting someone he doesn't know. But the law does not teach you to help someone. A leash does not teach a dog to help or be kind to someone whom it doesn't know. A Christian does not need a leash or a law. A Christian is taught to help and love everyone. That is real self-control.

Dogs need leashes. All people need the law to tell them what not to do, but the Christian needs self-control to teach him how to help and to love. A Christian will control himself and help others.

JESUS IS YOUR WEDGE

2 Corinthians 11:19-12:9, vs. 9a: "But he said to me, 'My grace is sufficient for you, for my power is made perfect in weakness.' "

Object: A nail, a board, a hammer, and a small piece of wood to be used as a wedge for pulling the nail out of board.

Good morning, boys and girls. When I look around here on a Sunday morning, I always think to myself that not only are you the best looking group in the world, but also the strongest. Do you feel strong? [*Let them answer.*] Of course, even the strongest must feel a little weak sometimes. If you have something to lift that is far too heavy for your size, then you feel weak compared to it. When that happens you need help. If you don't get the help then you fail at what you are doing.

Jesus claims that when we are weak in our faith, he will be a real strength to us, and help us to overcome our weakness. I want to show you what I mean by that. I am going to drive a nail into this big board and only leave a little bit of the head sticking out. [*Drive the nail.*] Now I am going to try to pull the nail. [*Pull it out but show how hard it is to do it.*] Now I am going to drive the nail again, only this time I am going to pull it out in a little different way. [*Drive the nail.*] If I take this board and put it under my hammer and then pull it out it will come much easier. [*Show them how to do it this way. If you have time you may let several children try it both ways.*]

The wedge board under the hammer helps overcome your weakness. By yourself it is hard, but with the help of the wedge it is much easier. That is the way that Jesus is with our faith. When we are weak and have trouble believing, we need to turn to Jesus and ask him for help. People have been doing this for years and have found that it really works. People who are sick or afraid turn to Jesus and Jesus helps them overcome whatever problem they have.

I know a lot of children who have questions about things that they find hard to believe and they are weak about it. Jesus says turn your questions and fears over to him and he will make everything all right. Jesus is like the wedge under the hammer. He makes life better when things are tough.

The next time you have to pull a nail out of a board you will remember to get a wedge and it will make that easier. The next time you have a problem or are afraid, you can turn it over to Jesus and he will solve it.

REPORTING ON LOVE

1 Corinthians 13:1-13, vs. 4-7: Love is patient and kind; love is not jealous or boastful; it is not arrogant or rude. Love does not insist on its own way; it is not irritable or resentful; it does not rejoice at wrong, but rejoices in the right. Love bears all things, believes all things, hopes all things, endures all things.

Object: A pad of paper and pencil and something to describe, such as a person, a picture or the chancel of the church.

Good morning, boys and girls. How would you like to be a newspaper reporter? Now, I don't mean a newspaper boy, but a real news reporter. Have you ever seen a reporter at work? I just love to watch the reporter write down what he hears and sees when he is at work. Let's choose a couple of you to be reporters and let you describe our church for everyone who has not seen it. You tell me what you see and I will write it down on this paper. [*Choose some reporters.*] Now, remember that you are telling this to people who have never been here, so you must include everything that you think is important. [*Let them tell you what they see and you write it down so that you can give the information back.*]

That was very good. I am sure that when people read what you have reported they will want to come here and be a part of our congregation. That is what a good reporter is supposed to do. He should make people be able to see what something is really like with the use of words.

St. Paul was a good reporter. If I asked you to tell me what love was, do you think that you could describe it? [*Let them answer.*] We feel love but it is pretty hard to describe. St. Paul described it in a letter to some Christians a long time ago, and no one has ever told about it any better. Paul was a good reporter because he knew what God's love was all about. I want to read to you just a small part of what he said and it will give you some idea of what a good reporter Paul was. [Read the above verses.] Do you understand what Paul reported? He reported on love and he described it in a way that no one would ever forget. It is hard to describe love, but Paul did it with the help of God. Love is what being a Christian is all about. Paul wrote about love so that we would all know what God is really like and what God wants us to be like.

Paul was a good reporter. The next time that you read a newspaper or see something that requires a reporter, I want you to think about St. Paul and his reporting about love.

DON'T BE A SPOON IN A GLASS

2 Corinthians 6:1-10, vs. 3: We put no obstacle in anyone's way, so that no fault may be found with our ministry.

Object: A glass of iced tea and an iced tea spoon.

Good morning, boys and girls. How are you today? I brought with me this morning a very refreshing drink. Do any of you ever drink iced tea? It is a delicious drink, especially if you add a little sugar and some lemon. I remember a long time ago when someone served me a glass of iced tea with a very fancy long iced tea spoon in the glass. I didn't know what to do about the spoon, since it looked like it belonged with the glass. I tried to drink the iced tea with this long spoon sticking out and it kept poking me in the eye and the cheek and the nose. Everyone thought that the way that I drank the glass of iced tea was pretty funny. I thought that the spoon was a terrible obstacle.

Do you know what an obstacle is? [*Let them answer.*] An obstacle is something that gets in your way. The iced tea spoon is an obstacle if you let it stay in the glass when you are trying to drink.

There are other kinds of obstacles and some of them are called people. People are sometimes obstacles when they keep other people from learning and knowing Jesus. Paul was very careful to say to us that people watch how Christians live and act and they decide if they want to be followers of our God by the way that we live. If we make them mad or unhappy or if we do things that hurt them like cheating or lying, then we are obstacles. We are just like that spoon that kept poking me in the face so long ago.

A Christian tries to be good for many reasons, but one of the best reasons is that he wants other people to think good things about his God. Anyone who knows our God will be glad that you taught him about him. The best way that you can teach others about Christianity is by being a Christian.

Don't be a spoon in a glass. Don't be an obstacle to someone who is trying to learn about God. If you are a Christian then live like a Christian and others will come to you to learn about being a follower of God.

THE MOST IMPORTANT INSTRUCTIONS IN THE WORLD

1 Thessalonians 4:1-7, vs. 2: For you know what instructions we gave you through the Lord Jesus.

Object: An income tax form with all of the instructions.

Good morning, boys and girls. Maybe I should have said good morning to all future taxpayers. Do any of you know anything about taxes? What are taxes? [*Let them answer.*] Does everybody pay them? [*Let them answer.*] It seems like almost everybody pays them except children. Taxes are something that we pay to our governments so that they have enough money to pay the workers, the men in the army, to make new roads and build bridges and a thousand other things. Most people do not like to pay taxes, but if we are to have schools and fire departments and things like that then we all have to pay taxes. How much do you pay? That is a hard question. Not everybody pays the same. As a matter of fact, that is what our lesson is about this morning. I brought with me an instruction book on how to pay your taxes so that you will know how much you have to pay. Just look at it. Your parents are looking at things like this all of the time and they wonder how they will ever understand it. There are certain laws for taxes, and the instructions are supposed to help us know what it is all about.

That isn't the only book of instructions. St. Paul told us that the Scriptures were written for our instruction and that they are to be read and understood. I don't think that the Bible is as complicated as a tax form, but then God is able to tell us a little more simply what he wants us to know and learn than the men who write the taxes are able to. The Bible is also written for everybody. No one is left out of the Bible, including children. Children don't need to know much about the tax book and the instructions, but they should know a lot about the Bible.

Now St. Paul wrote other Christians about the instructions that Jesus left with him and told him to share with others. I know that you have heard about them many times when you come to church and Sunday School, and I want you to know that they are the most important instructions that you will ever get. Nothing else is so important as the instructions that Jesus gives about living. When he tells you to love your neighbor and forgive those who hurt you, he is giving you the best news and way to live that you will ever hear. That is what I mean about instructions.

When you see your mom and dad working with their tax instructions, you know that they are working with some very important instructions. When they get the Bible out and read it to you, then you know that you are also getting instructions and you also know that these are the most important in the world.

WALKING IS EASIER

Ephesians 5:1-9, vs. 2: And walk in love, as Christ loved us and gave himself up for us, a fragrant offering and sacrifice to God.

Object: Select some children to hop, some to skip, some to jump, and some, if you like, to run. [This can all be done in place.]

Good morning, boys and girls. How are you today? How many of you like to run, jump, skip, hop, and crawl? I am going to ask each of you to do one of those things that I mentioned. [*Select a jumper, hopper, skipper, etc.*] Now, I don't want you to run through the church, so I am going to ask you to run or skip or hop in place like I am doing. [*Demonstrate running in place.*] Now, I want you to do this while I am talking to you so that you will understand what I am trying to show you. The Bible talks about walking in love and I wondered why it never speaks about hopping in love, or running in love, or skipping in love, or any of the other ways that we move. I think that hopping is a lot of fun, and I thought that maybe if the people in the Bible knew how much we liked to hop, they would rewrite the Bible so that all of us could enjoy our love a little more.

Is anyone getting a little tired of hopping or jumping or doing anything that you are doing? When you get tired you are allowed to stop whatever you are doing. As you stop I want to tell you that I now understand why the Bible talked about walking in love rather than running or jumping or hopping. Do you know why? [*Let them answer.*] The reason I think the Bible talks about walking is that we can do that for a long time, all day if we wanted to, while we can only run or hop or jump for a short time. God wants us to have love for a long time and to use it always. He doesn't want us to start and stop loving every few seconds. That is why he talks about walking in love and not running.

We think that love is such a real part of being a Christian that we try to tell people they should try loving all of the time. Love your neighbors, your friends, your family, and even your enemies, for that is the way that Christ taught us to live. Walking you can do all day, but the other things are only for a short time. Love all of the time and let your other feelings be only for a moment. That is the way God teaches us, and that is the way we want to be.

THE OLD WAY AND THE NEW WAY

Galatians 4:21-5:1a, vs. 24a: Now this true story is an illustration of God's two ways of helping people.

Object: A safety razor and an electric razor.

Good morning, boys and girls. Did you know that God is interested in helping people? We hear a lot about the way that we can help God, but did you know that God likes to help people? Of course you did. The Bible teaches us that God has two ways of helping people. He works two ways to do the same thing. Do you know two ways to do the same thing? [*Let them answer.*] I thought a lot about this, and I know of something that I do every morning that can be done in two different ways. How many of you have ever watched someone shave? Do you know the two ways that I am talking about? [*Let them reply.*] That's right, you can shave with a safety razor or you can shave with an electric razor.

Not too long ago people always shaved with soap and water or shaving cream and a safety razor. To shave this way you have to get your face ready with hot water and then the shaving cream. [*You can put a little of the shaving cream in the hand of each child.*] This is the old way, and some people still like to do it this way. Then after men discovered electricity and how to use it, they started making things like electric razors. [*Run an electric razor over the palm of each child's hand.*] Some people started using this kind of razor and have never gone back to the old way. It seemed a lot easier and they could do it without cutting themselves or using a lot of hot water. It was a second way to do the same thing.

God has two ways to help people. There is the law which includes the Ten Commandments. It tells people what to do and when to do it and how much to do. The

Law is the old way and the hard way, because it always asks something of you that you can hardly do. There is a new way. That way is to believe that Jesus is God's Son and that he did everything for you. Now instead of trying to keep a law, you simply live to love others the way that Jesus loves you.

Let me try to explain it one other way. If you follow the law, the old way, then you are trying very hard to work your way into heaven all by yourself. If you take the new way, then you are asking that Jesus do the work which he already has done so that he will take you with him into heaven. These are the two ways that God has of helping people. God has a Law and God has a Son. Christians have taken the New Way to follow Jesus and have left the Law for those who do not follow Jesus. We are glad to have the new way and to love others as Jesus has already loved us.

JESUS, THE RESCUER

Hebrews 9:11-15: Christ came with this new agreement so that all who are invited may come and have forever all the wonders God has promised them. For Christ died to rescue them from the penalty of the sins they had committed while still under that old system.

Object: A rope or some piece of rescue equipment.

Good morning, boys and girls. How many of you have ever thought that you would like to be a fireman or a policeman or a member of the rescue squad? [*Let them answer.*] It would be fun and also good for us to help people in dangerous situations. I think that all of us would like to be brave and help other people, wouldn't we? I brought with me this morning something that all of you have seen. What do you call this thing that I have in my hand? [*Let them answer.*] That's right, a rope. But it is not just an ordinary rope. No sir, this is a piece of rope that is used to rescue people. This is the kind of rope that is used to help people who are drowning or are trapped in a fire. Without this rope a lot of people would have been hurt worse than they were. This rope helped to rescue someone who was in real trouble. Of course, it took a man to hold on to the other end, but the rope helped to rescue the person who needed help.

The Bible teaches us about another rescue that we are all a part of along with Jesus. The man who wrote the book of Hebrews said that Jesus rescued us from death. Did you hear that? He rescued us. That sounds exciting, doesn't it? Usually people say that Jesus saved us, but the writer of Hebrews said that he rescued us. Where were we that we needed to be rescued and what from? Were we in a fire, or were we drowning, or what was happening that we needed to be rescued? Do you know? [*Let them answer.*] We were rescued from death because of our sins. You know that the penalty for sin is living without God and away from God. Jesus came to us and rescued us from being alone and being punished. Jesus took our sins and suffered with them instead of letting us suffer. He paid the penalty and we are now free to live with God here on earth and in heaven. That is what God did for us through Jesus. He rescued us.

Now the next time that you see a rope or any piece of rescue equipment, you can think about how Jesus rescued us when he died on the cross. Jesus paid the penalty so that we could be free. We say, "Thanks be to God for sending his Son into the world to rescue us from being hurt or paying the penalty."

BRAGGERS

John 8:46-59, vs. 54: Then Jesus told them this. "If I am merely boasting about myself, it doesn't count. But it is my Father — and you claim him as your God — who is saying these glorious things about me." [L. B.]

Object: A magazine or newspaper advertisement that boldly proclaims the super value of some product.

Good morning, boys and girls. How are you today? I brought something that we are getting very used to — something which I am sure that you have seen before. [*Hold up the advertisement. Read it with great expression so that the children understand that you are boasting about whatever product you are selling.*] Have you ever heard someone on TV or radio sell something so that it sounded as if he were boasting? When people talk in a loud voice about themselves or about something that belongs to them, we stop listening or turn them off so that we do not have to listen. No one likes to hear someone brag or boast about himself.

On the other hand, I am very interested in hearing about a tire or a kind of soap if the person talking about it doesn't own it, or is not trying to sell it. For instance, suppose that I told you that I used a certain kind of soap in my washing machine and it got my clothes cleaner than any other kind of soap I have ever used. The next time you or someone in your family buys soap, you will probably want to try that kind. I am not talking about a soap that I make or sell, but I am talking about a kind of soap that I have used that is good for me.

The reason I tell you this is that this is how we know that Jesus is the Lord. Jesus told us that he wouldn't expect you or me to believe him if he said that he was the Lord. It is not Jesus who tells us this, but God the Father in heaven who says that Jesus is Lord and

Savior. That's different. It is not Jesus who is boasting, but the Father who is telling us that this Jesus is his Son and the Saviour of all. Jesus did not boast or brag about being God, but the Father said he was, and that makes a lot of difference.

The next time you hear someone bragging about something that he did you may think about this. When someone brags it is not too important, but when someone else tells you how good another person is, then you believe it. The same is true about Jesus. He never told anyone or bragged to anyone about who he was, but his Father in heaven told us that Jesus was his Son and that means something very important. It means that the things that we hear about him are true and should always be believed.

GOD'S WONDERFUL DISGUISE

Philippians 2:5-11, vs. 7: But laid aside his mighty power and glory, taking the disguise of a slave and becoming like men.

Object: A candle that is shaped to represent something else [A clock or an animal, or anything BUT a candle.]

Good morning, boys and girls. How many of you know what a disguise is? [*Let them answer.*] Have you ever worn a disguise? Did anyone know you when you wore your disguise? I know that they didn't. Wearing a disguise is fun sometimes, and other times it is necessary. Here is one of the fun times. I want you to tell me what you think that I have here in my hand. [*Hold up the candle and see who can guess that it is a candle.*] Did you think it was a clock? It looks like a clock, but if you look carefully you will see that the hands do not move, nor can you hear it tick-tock. The disguise is a clock but what is it really? Does anyone know? It's a candle. That's right, it is a candle that is disguised as a clock.

The Bible teaches us that Jesus, according to the plan of his Father in Heaven, came in disguise to earth so that he could be like other men. It was the plan of God to come and work and serve like other men so that people like you and me would treat him like a man. God could have come with mighty power and changed us like magic, but that was not the plan. God wanted to come to earth but he needed a disguise. He could have come as a tree or a tiger or anything that he wanted, but since he wanted to show men how much he loved them, he came as a man and lived here as a man.

Isn't it great to know that God loved us so much that he chose to be a man? That was a great disguise because no one ever knew that Jesus was God until the time that he died and was resurrected. People thought that he was a marvelous doctor, a great teacher, and a tremendous preacher, but no one thought that he was God. This was his disguise, just as the clock was a disguise for the candle.

The next time that you see something disguised you can think about the wonderful disguise that God used so that he could work with men and bring them salvation.

GOD'S ORDER

1 Corinthians 15:20-26, vs. 23: Each, however, in his own turn: Christ rose first; then when Christ comes back, all his people will become alive again.

Object: A set of cards with numbers on it from one to ten, or a variety of numbers that the children can put in order.

Good morning, boys and girls. A very happy Easter to you. The best day of the whole church year is here and we can all celebrate together. Jesus Christ is risen today! He is not dead but alive! They did all of the things they wanted to do to him, including the worst of all — crucifixion — and today he is alive! The people in the Bible shouted, "Hallelujah, Hallelujah, Christ is risen from the dead." Isn't that a joyous sound? We should do that ourselves. Let's all say it together. "Hallelujah, Hallelujah, Christ is risen from the dead!" Doesn't that make your heart jump and your feet feel like running? I know that it is the way I feel.

But what does this mean for you and me? Why should we be so happy that Jesus is alive, and they could not kill him? [Let them answer.] I'll tell you why. We are going to live again, too, just as Jesus did. Did you know that? Well, it's true. Let me show you what I mean.

I have some cards with numbers written on them. I am going to lay them down and I want you to put them in the right order. [Take out the cards and read the numbers in a very mixed up order.] Now, I want you to start with the smallest number and put them in a line until the last one is the largest number. [Allow them a few seconds to do this.] There is a certain order that is right and it would not work any other way.

The same thing is true about the idea that the first one to come back to life after he died was to be Jesus.

Now the Bible says that there will be one more thing happen before other people who die shall come back to life. This other thing is that Jesus must return to earth again, and when he comes back all of the people who believe in him will also be brought back to life. That is the order God has set. There is only one way, just as there is only one way to arrange the numbers.

Just think, part of it has already happened. Jesus is risen from the dead. Now all we are waiting for is for him to come back to earth as he promised. Then we will all be taken with him to a wonderful place that we call heaven or God's Eternal Kingdom. It is nice to know that God works in a good order so that we can count on him and know what there is to expect. If you can put numbers in order, you can also know what the order is that God has made for us to join Jesus in heaven.

JESUS' WITNESS

1 John 5:4-12, vs. 9: We use men as witnesses in our courts, and so we can surely believe what God tells us. And God has said that Jesus is his Son.

Object: A series of newspaper photographs that depict different events that have transpired during the week. [An Easter egg hunt, a victory celebration, etc.]

Good morning, boys and girls. Here we are, one week since Easter and the thrill of it is still with us. I hope that you remember the great story about how Jesus was resurrected from the grave and how he promised that the same thing would be shared with us. Some people wonder how that can happen, and what proof do we have that it will be that way for us.

I hope that I can show you why we can believe that Jesus is the Son of God and how we can take the promise that he made to us. This morning I have some pictures that were taken out of the newspaper. Let's look at them. [*Have the pictures cut out and show them one at a time.*] Here is a picture of the Easter Egg Hunt that was taken last week. Were any of you there? The picture is a witness of that event. Now here is one of the grand champion dog at the Dog Show last Wednesday night. The picture is a witness that this dog was made the champion. Here is another picture of two people who were elected to be leaders of the clubs that they belong to. The picture is a witness to that event. Every picture in the paper is a witness to something that happened this past week in our town or some place in the world. Pictures are witnesses.

In the day Jesus lived, there were no pictures taken with cameras. But one of the writers in the Bible remembered some other witnesses who were even more important than the witnesses of pictures. This writer remembered when God spoke and said in a loud, clear voice that Jesus was his Son. He remembered when Jesus was baptized that a voice from heaven said, "This is my Son." That is a pretty good witness and one that could not be forgotten.

This is the reason that men like John believed. They believed not because of what men said as witnesses, but from what they remembered that God said. This was the witness for Jesus, and it is the best witness that anyone has ever had. We have pictures and tape recordings and things like that which are witnesses for things that happen to us, but Jesus had the voice of God and the witness no one could doubt.

If God said that Jesus is his Son and that we will live again the way that Jesus lived again, then we can believe it. I promise you that you can count on the one who made a witness for Jesus, for that witness was God.

LOADED DOWN

1 Peter 2:21b-25, vs. 24: He personally carried the load of our sins in his own body when he died on the cross; so that we can be finished with sin, and live from now on for all that is good. For his wounds have healed ours!

Object: A child's coat and hat, some dishes, clothes, some wood for the fireplace, school books and groceries.

Good morning, boys and girls. How are you today? Have you had a good week? Have you had any complaints or problems with people that you have not been able to take care of with a little bit of attention? No problems? Everything is pretty good? That's wonderful.

I brought along some problems I know you have, and I thought that we might talk about them. I asked some parents about the problems children have and they made a list for me so that I could pass them around and share them with all of you. First of all, I have the old problem of the coat and hat. What do we do with a coat and hat? It seems so hard to hang up and so easy to throw on a chair, on a lamp or on the floor. It's a problem that all kids have. Then there is the problem with dirty dishes. No one seems to like doing dishes. While we are talking about things that are dirty, there are your clothes that seem to hang around and show up in the strangest places. Then there is the firewood, the carrying of school books, and helping carry in the groceries. These are real problems. How many of you see your problem? Now suppose that you had someone who would come along and say to you that he would take care of all of these problems? Wouldn't that be great? Can you imagine never having to do another dish or carry a book or help carry the groceries? I think that would be wonderful. Think how good life would be if you did not have those problems.

Suppose that I agreed to take on all of your problems. [*Carry them all in your hands and arms so that you are really loaded down with wood, dishes, etc.*] Wouldn't it be great if I could go with each one of you and do your dishes and pick up your coat and dirty clothes? You would not have a problem in the world.

I can't do that, but it will help me to tell you about another kind of help that you have that you have forgotten about. Do you ever think about your sins and how much you should worry about the things that you have done that are wrong? Why don't you worry? I know why. You do not have to worry. Jesus tells us that he will carry all of the load when it comes to sins. No matter what you have done if you ask him, he will carry the whole load. That's the truth. He is better than any other problem solver I know. Jesus will carry your load of sin just as I would like to solve your problems, only he can do it and I cannot. If you have a sin and you want to get rid of it then take it to Jesus and he will carry it for you and you can forget all about it. That is what it means when people tell you that Jesus forgives all sin and loves you for giving them up to him.

A VISIT TO GOD

1 Peter 2:11-20, vs. 11: Dear brothers, you are only visitors here. Since your real home is in heaven I beg you to keep away from the evil pleasures of this world; they are not for you, for they fight against your very soul.

Object: Several suitcases.

Good morning, boys and girls. I could have called you visitors since the Bible talks about you as visitors. That's right, the Bible calls you visitors so I am going to call you visitors today. I brought along something that every person should have if he is going to be a good visitor. [*Bring out the suitcases.*] How many of you have a suitcase that you take with you when you visit somewhere? [*Let them answer.*] That is very good.

What do you do with your suitcase? [*Let them answer.*] You pack it with clothes and other things that you will need, like your toothbrush and comb. Who do you visit? [*Let them answer.*] You visit your friends and relatives. Visiting is fun. As a matter of fact, I would say that visiting is exciting. But when your visit is over you like to go home. There is no place like home.

The Bible teaches us that we are visitors here in this world. We may live here for a hundred years, but we are still visitors because our real home is with God. Christians live out of a suitcase the whole time that they live on earth. We are visitors because God promises us that there is another place — a real place — that we shall call home. Another word for this home that God makes for us is heaven. When we are through with our visit here on earth then we shall go home to heaven. Isn't that a wonderful thought? Someday we will all die and when we die we will not be leaving home but instead we shall be going back home where God is waiting for us.

The next time you see a suitcase or even talk about going somewhere for a visit, you can think about this lesson that you learned today. A visit to your friends is like living here on earth. Going home to your house will be like going home to God and living with him in heaven. It will be nice to know that when we live with God we will not have to live out of a suitcase but instead he will have a real place for us to stay and live forever.

WEEDS IN YOUR LIFE

James 1:17-21, vs. 21: So get rid of all that is wrong in your life, both inside and outside, and humbly be glad for the wonderful message we have received, for it is able to save our souls as it grows in our hearts.

Object: A dandelion.

Good morning, boys and girls. Today we have a real fooler for you. At least it fools me. Every spring when I look out in my yard and I see some beautiful yellow flowers growing in my yard, I think how beautiful they look and how I would like to have a whole field of them. These beautiful things look like this. [*Hold up dandelion.*]

How many of you know what I have here? That's right, and I call the dandelion a fooler. Do you know why? [*Let them answer.*] It's a weed and what is so awful about a weed? I will tell you what is so awful about a weed. They are greedy. They will not let anything else grow by them. They kill other plants and choke them in such a way that if you do not get rid of them they will take over your whole yard. Now how do you get rid of a dandelion? Can you cut them off with a lawnmower? No, and you can't get rid of them any other way that just chops off the head and the part you can see above the ground. If you want to get rid of a dandelion you must get rid of both the parts that you can see and the parts that you cannot see under the ground.

Getting rid of weeds is a lot like getting rid of sin. There are two parts of sin and you must get rid of them both. There is the part that you can see or hear, like the lie that you tell. We all know that a lie is wrong, and when we tell it or hear it told we want to get rid of it right away. That is the easy part. But we also have to get rid of the part that we cannot see. We have to get rid of the reason that we lied and that reason is deep in our heart. We lied because we wanted to hurt someone or because we were afraid. If you want to make sure that you are not going to lie again you must get rid of the hate or the fear that is in your heart. A sin is like the dandelion. There is the part that you can see and the part that you cannot see, and both must be gotten rid of if you are to have a good life.

When I see a yard without any weeds, I know that someone has given a lot of care to the grass and has worked hard to give the plants plenty of room to grow. When I see a life of someone without a lot of wrong in it, I know that someone has taken a lot of care to get rid of both parts of a sin. He not only looks good on the outside, but he is also clean on the inside. I hope that you have a life that is free of wrong, just as I hope that your yard doesn't have any weeds!

GETTING BACK WHAT YOU PUT IN

2 Corinthians 9:6-10, vs. 6: *But remember this, that if you give little you will get little. A farmer who plants just a few seeds will get only a small crop, but if he plants much, he will reap much.*

Object: A list of facts about yourself. You give only one fact to the first child, two to the next, three to the third, etc.

Good morning, boys and girls. I am going to play a game with you today to see how sharp you are at listening and remembering. How many of you like to play games? I love to play games. In this game I am going to tell you something about myself and I want you to see how much you can remember to tell everybody. [*Begin with the first one and tell him your name, then go to the second one and tell him the name of the street that you live on. The third one can be told your age and the fourth one your favorite sport and the name of your home town. Now each one of them should be given the total amount of information so that the last one has all of the facts while the first one will know only your name and nothing else.*]

Now let's begin. I want to see what all of you know about me. [*Begin with the first one whom you told your secret to and build it up from there.*] That's my name! Is there anything else that you can tell me about myself? That's all you know. Well, let us go on to the second person and see what he remembers. You know my name and where I live. [*Speaking to the first person.*] You only knew my name, but she knows my name and where I live. Let's see if anyone else knows anything different about me. [*Get the information from each child until you have completed the whole group.*] Why does the last person know more about me than the rest of you? [*Let them answer.*] That's right, because I told her more about me than I told the rest of you. I got more information back from her because I gave more information to her.

This isn't anything new. You always get more back when you put more in to what you are doing. St. Paul talked about people and the way they give, and he said that God loved cheerful givers. He also said that people who give a lot of themselves to God will receive a lot back from God. This isn't a special deal, but just the way that God works in the world. If you want to share what you have with God, then he will have you to share with; but if you want to keep everything that you have to yourself, God will not be able to share with you. That is why we worked this morning with the information so that you could see that the person who was given the most could also share the most. When you have a chance to share with God the things that you have, then he will also share with you. Give God a lot of yourself, and he will be able to give a lot of himself to you.

OUR SPECIAL GIFT

1 Peter 4:7b-11, vs. 10: God has given each of you some special abilities; be sure to use them, to help each other, passing on to others God's many kinds of blessings.

Object: As many different people with different talents as you can assemble.

Good morning, boys and girls. I am always pleased to see you on Sunday morning and to see how different all of you look. There is no mistaking one of you for the other unless you have a twin. Each of you has something different about you that lets me remember who you are and what you can do. That's the way I remember your parents and friends, too. Let's take a look at some of the members of our congregation.

[*Begin to introduce the members by name and vocation. Say something very important about each one of them and emphasize how different the work is that each of them does.*] We could go on and on talking about the things that all of our members do in our town. Did you know that there are over 750,000 different kinds of work?

The Christian is thankful to God that he has given us so many ways to serve him and each other. God gives us all of these different talents so that we can help each other live better in this world. The doctor could be his own carpenter and build a house, and be a teacher and teach his own children. But then, think of how little doctoring he would do. While he was teaching his children, you would have to suffer with your sore throat and earache.

God knew all about that kind of thinking, and he gave each of us a talent that was so special that we would need each other. When you are needed and you help the person who needs you, then you make that person glad. God knew that and wanted us to need each other, so he gave us this special gift. I hope that you will find out about your talent and use it to make other people happy. When you are a blessing to people you are pleasing to God.

A WINDY BIRTHDAY

Acts 2:1-11, vs. 2: Suddenly there was a sound like the roaring of a mighty windstorm in the skies above them and it filled the house where they were meeting.

Object: Have the children blow through their hands and make the sound of the wind.

Good morning, boys and girls. Today we are going to have some fun and talk about something that happened a long time ago that is really important to us today. The first thing that we have to do is practice making a big wind. I want everyone to blow through his hands until he sounds like a wind. No whistling, only blowing. [*Let them practice for a few seconds until you have a major sounding wind.*] That's very good. Now when I point to you I want you to make a sound like the wind.

This all happened one day after Jesus had gone back to his Father in heaven. Jesus had promised all the disciples that he would not leave them alone and that when he left he would send the Holy Spirit to share with them. It was a day like today, nothing too strange at all, when things began to happen. The disciples were all meeting together when they heard the strangest noise. [*Point to the children to make wind noises.*] The noise got louder and louder until the disciples were afraid to stay in the house for fear that it would blow down with them inside. All of a sudden they looked around and noticed that there were little tongues of fire dancing around the room and on the heads of other disciples. The wind grew so loud that the disciples ran down the stairs and out into the street.

Once they were outside, the wind died down [*Have the children grow quieter*], and they began to speak. But they did not just speak as usual, they spoke in different languages. They spoke in every language known to man. The amazing thing about this was that the languages that they spoke were languages which they had never spoken or known about before.

This was the visit of the Holy Spirit that Jesus had promised. Jesus had told them that the Spirit would do wonderful things with them, and Jesus was right. This is how it happened on the first Christian Pentecost, a day that no one has ever forgotten. Pentecost is the birthday of the Church. The next time you hear a big wind or see some dancing tongues of fire, you can remember what I told you about the day that God the Holy Spirit came to earth and visited the disciples.

GOD'S NOT A SALESMAN

Romans 11:33-36, vs. 35: And who has ever given anything to the Lord first as payment for something in return?

Object: Some marbles, crayons, trading cards, birthday money and a candy bar.

Good morning, boys and girls. I have a real problem today. I hope you can help me out of my terrible situation. I have tried for a long time to make God understand what I want, and I am not doing very well. There is something that I want very much, and I have offered to pay God in advance so that when it comes up he will remember me. Do you understand? I will give him something now if he will give me what I want later on. I have offered him almost everything I have. First, I took my marbles to bed with me and told God in prayer that I would give him my marbles, including my very best shooter. That didn't work. Since then I have offered to give him my crayons, some of my very best trading cards, and a candy bar. It still didn't work. Today I brought my birthday money that I got from my family, and I even told God that I would give him this if he would only promise to give me what I want. I asked him early this morning when I first got here, but I still have not heard a thing about it. What do you think is the problem? Do you have any help or ideas for me? [*Let them answer.*]

Have any of you ever tried to pay God for something that you really wanted? [*Let them answer.*] Some of you don't think that we can pay God. Why not? Everyone else likes to get paid. Why not God? Is it because God already has everything he needs? Maybe. But even more important is the idea that you cannot buy anything from God. He gives us everything that we need and doesn't charge us a thing. God is the giver, a good giver. Everything that he gives, he gives without charge or pay.

You cannot buy anything from God and neither can anyone else. God has given us everything that we have, and he gave it all to us for nothing. He also gives us the things that we need when we need them. Now I know why my candy bars, marbles, birthday money and crayons didn't work. I can keep them or share them with someone else, but God doesn't want me to buy anything from him. God wants to give me the things that are good for me.

GOD'S GUARANTEE

1 John 1:1-4, vs. 2a: This One who is Life from God has been shown to us and we guarantee that we have seen him . . .

Object: Some form of guarantee or warranty.

Good morning, boys and girls. How many of you have ever heard of the phrase, "a sure thing?" When something is a sure thing you know that you can count on it. Sometimes we call a sure thing a guarantee. Lots of stores give guarantees because they want people to buy things and know that what they have bought will last them a long time. When you buy a [*Use whatever your guarantee is for*] you receive a guarantee. I bought one of these at a store and was given a guarantee. If anything should ever happen to it, then I will simply give the store the guarantee and the store will replace what I bought with a new one.

The apostles wanted to show people that they knew who Jesus was and why they believed in him, so they guaranteed everyone that they had seen Jesus with their own eyes. They were ready to put their word on the line. The people believed what was told them to be true, and if they found out differently they would never have to believe another word the apostles said. "Jesus is from God," they said. They could guarantee it because they saw what he could do with their own eyes.

This was not something that they had heard from someone else. It was true because they saw it and they knew that it was true. This is the guarantee that we count on a lot because we know that we are not going to see Jesus with our own eyes or hear his voice with our own ears. We are counting on the guarantee of Peter and John and Paul and Matthew. These men and others were the witnesses of Jesus and they guarantee us that they saw all of the things that they have written about.

We like guarantees when they come from stores or from the Bible. This guarantee is in the Bible, and we believe in Jesus because of what they have told us and the love that the Holy Spirit has given us.

WHAT IS A CHRISTIAN CHECKBOOK?

1 John 3:13-18, vs. 17: But if someone who is supposed to be a Christian has money enough to live well, and sees a brother in need, and won't help him — how can God's love be within him?

Object: Checkbook.

Good morning, boys and girls. Today we are going to talk about our Christian checkbook. Did you know that there was a Christian checkbook? [*Let them answer.*] There are two kinds of checkbooks and sometimes people forget about having the Christian kind of checkbook. The other kind of checkbook is the kind that most people have. This kind of checkbook is for all of the things that I need and for no one else. This other kind of checkbook buys groceries and clothes, and pays the rent. It will also pay for a vacation, ball games, movies, restaurant dinners, new televisions and grass seed for the yard. It is a very valuable checkbook, and it is the kind that most people have.

The Christian checkbook does all of the things that the other one does, and then some other things as well. It buys food for some people who are not members of the family but who are hungry, and it takes care of the same people who do not have good clothing or a place to live. The Christian checkbook buys bandages for those who are ill, and bus tickets for those who must travel and do not have a way.

It isn't easy to have a Christian checkbook, but then it isn't easy to have money. When God gives you money he also gives you the responsibility to use it wisely. Of course, God has given us everything and he teaches us to share it with others, but that is not always easy to do. After we receive the things we do from God, it is hard to give them up and share them with others. We begin to think that everything we have belongs to us and to no one else. That is when we forget about the Christian checkbook and we use only the other kind. Coming to church and seeing other people without as much as we have are good reminders of the kind of checkbook that we should have. But we have to learn before we get checkbooks. You cannot wait until you have a checkbook to learn how to share. You must begin now so that when you grow up and God gives you a lot of responsibility and money to go with it, you will remember which kind of a checkbook you are going to keep and use at your house.

Will you remember that? I'm sure you will.

USE THE BEST SWEEPER

Romans 8:18-23, vs. 18: Yet what we suffer now is nothing compared to the glory he will give us later.

Object: A broom and a vacuum sweeper.

Good morning, boys and girls. Today we are going to talk about what it will be like to live with God in heaven as compared with the way that we live with him now. I would not want you to think that you are going to have to wait until you die to know God and to know that God is with you right now. As a matter of fact, I can tell you that you have a pretty good life with God just the way it is today. But will it get any better? Let me show you what I think about this.

I have with me two kinds of sweepers. They are both supposed to pick up dust and dirt off your carpets. [*Use the broom.*] A broom is one kind of sweeper, and it works pretty well. This is like the life that we have here on earth. There is nothing wrong with the broom, and when that is all that you have you think it is pretty good. It doesn't get way down into the carpet and pick up the dust that is deep, but it makes the carpet look pretty good. The other problem with the broom is that it makes a lot of dust, and in a little while the dust will come back and lie on the carpet, and under the carpet. Our lives here on earth are kind of like that. Most of our days are pretty good. There is nothing to complain about most of the time, but sometimes we are sick, sometimes we are very sick, sometimes we are unhappy and we have problems that make us wish that we had never even seen each other. That is when our lives are like a broom.

But here is another way to sweep your carpet. [*Take out the big vacuum sweeper and plug it in.*] Now when you sweep your carpet with this big machine you know that you are going to get it clean. It not only picks up the dirt on top, but it also picks up the dust that is underneath and removes it so that it will never come back again. When you have cleaned with this sweeper you have done the job.

There is no comparison which is the better sweeper. The last one does the complete job. That is the way that our life with God in heaven will be. It will be complete and there will be no sickness or unhappiness. Being with God is the best and it can not be compared with anything. That is why I want you to know that God is looking forward to our coming with him because he wants us to have life with him as he enjoys it now.

ONLY JESUS CAN DO IT

Romans 6:3-11, vs. 3b: Through his death the power of your sinful nature was shattered.

Object: Some soda crackers.

Good morning, boys and girls. Today we want to talk a little about sin. Sin is not a very pleasant subject, and sometimes we wish that we could stop talking about it and perhaps it would go away. A lot of people have tried that, but it doesn't work. There is only one way to get rid of sin, and that is what we are going to talk about this morning.

Sin is hard to get rid of, and it is even harder on you. Sin hurts. It makes different people out of us from what we would like to be. Most of the people I know would like to get away from sin if they knew how to do it. Can you think of some ways to get rid of sin? [*Let them answer.*] It is hard to think of how we can get rid of it. The Bible talks a lot about getting rid of sin, but it also knows only one way to get rid of it that works. Let me tell you about it.

Sin is something that is within us, and Jesus is the only answer to sin. The Bible says that Jesus shattered sin. Do you know what shattering means? [*Let them answer.*] I have some crackers with me, and I want to show you what shattering means. [*Lay the crackers down on a table and either hit them with your fist or some object like a hammer.*] The crackers are shattered. That means that they are broken into little bits. There are no crackers that are whole or even look like the crackers used to look. Jesus does to sin what the hammer did to the crackers. He breaks the sin up so that it no longer looks or acts as it used to. You cannot have both sin and Jesus within your heart. Jesus is too strong for sin, and when you let Jesus into your heart then the sin is shattered. It simply crumbles up and washes away. When sin sees Jesus coming it tries to run and hide, but Jesus will not let it go away. Instead the power of Jesus is used and he shatters the sin into a million pieces.

That is why it is so important to have Jesus come into your life. There is no other way to get rid of the sin. The only way is to destroy it, and Jesus is the only one who can do it. The next time you take a soda cracker and crumble it all up, I want you to think about the way that Jesus shatters sin, and then you will be glad that you have Jesus in your heart instead of sin.

YOUR OWN KNOB

1 Peter 3:8-15a, vs. 10: If you want a happy, good life, keep control of your tongue, and guard your lips from telling lies.

Object: A radio.

Good morning, boys and girls. How are you today? Do you have control of yourself? Do you know what I mean when I ask you if you have control? [*Let them answer.*] Jesus and his followers thought that control was very important in being a Christian. There is one part of our body that they thought needed more control than almost any other. Do you know what part I am talking about? [*Let them guess.*] We use this part almost more than any other part of our body. Now do you know what I mean? That's right, the tongue. We really need to control it or it gets out of hand. Let me show you what I mean.

[*Have the radio plugged in, the pre-set at its loudest point.*] I have a radio with me and I am going to plug it in so that we can listen to it. How do you like that for a radio? It's a little hard to hear what you are saying when I have my radio on so loud. That is the reason I do not have it plugged in all the time. It would be nice if I could talk to you and also play my radio, but the radio seems a little loud for me to hear you. I know that you feel the same way, but it is all I can do to talk over the radio let alone listen to you. Do you have any suggestions? [*Wait for someone to turn it down or suggest that you turn it down.*] Did you say turn it down? That's a good idea, but how do I do it? Maybe one of these knobs will work. I suppose that you call this a control knob. [*Turn the radio down.*] Now that is what I call control!

Wouldn't it be wonderful if I could have the same kind of control over my tongue? We should be able to if we want to have a happy life. Jesus taught all of his disciples the value of having good control over their tongues, and he argued the same thing for us.

We don't have knobs but we do have minds that tell us when we are talking too much, or when we are saying something bad, or telling lies. Our minds are all the control we need if we believe in Jesus. So the next time you see a radio and turn it up or down, think about the kind of control you must have over your tongue and be glad that you do, so that you can have a happy life.

THE WORRY SACK

1 Peter 5:6-11, vs. 7: *Let him have all your worries and cares, for he is always thinking about you and watching everything that concerns you.*

Object: *Paper sacks [some of different sizes]. If possible have one for each child.*

Good morning, boys and girls. I am going to share something with you this morning that will be a help to you all of your life if you use it. I know that it works because I have tried it and I think that it is just great. First of all, I want to show you what I have and then I will tell you how to use it.

[*Hold up the paper sack.*] This is a paper sack, the same kind that you get whenever you go to the grocery. This sack is a lot more important than it looks. I call it my worry sack. This is how I use it. Every night before I go to bed I think about the things that have worried me during the day and the things that are going to worry me before I fall asleep. I write out my worries and put them in the worry sack. Then do you know what I do? I give my worry sack to God. God gets all of my worries. I sleep so much better without worries that I do this every night. Sometimes I give God the same worry and sometimes he gets a brand new worry.

I saved all of the worries that I had last night so that I could show you this morning what a worry sack is like. [*Begin to pull out some slips of paper with worries written on them.*] Here are some worries that a lot of people have to worry about. "How shall I pay that bill that I owe the dentist when he wants to be paid?" "I wonder if my friend John will forgive me for what I said about him to Bill?" Have you ever said something about somebody and worried that he might find out and think bad things about you? I have a lot of other worries written down like the repairs that need to be made on the car and the things that I should say at my appointment tomorrow. They are all in the sack. God is going to work on them so that I don't have to worry.

I can think of only one thing at a time and when I am worrying I cannot help anyone or do anything that is good for people. I must let God take over my worries and I must do the things that God wants me to do. One of the things that God does not want me to do is worry, so I put them into a sack and let God take care of them.

This is a wonderful system, and it works. Besides that, I am doing just what the Bible teaches me to do since it tells me to turn all of my worries over to God and he will take care of them. I have a worry sack for each of you. I hope that you will take it home and use it. Let God take care of your worries and you take care of the things that he has asked you to do.

A MUDDY RAG

Romans 6:19-23, vs. 21: And what was the result? Evidently not good since you are ashamed now even to think about those things you used to do, for all of them end in eternal doom.

Object: A rag with mud on it.

Good morning, boys and girls. I wonder if there is anyone here who knows what it is to be ashamed? Can you remember the last time that you were ashamed for something that you did or said? I want to show you something that I found hidden in a corner of my house and I suspect that I know where it came from. [*Take out the muddy rag.*] I know a little boy who was supposed to take good care of his new shoes and not get mud on them. I knew that this certain little boy was gone for a little while but when I asked him where he had been he just told me that he "was around." Now I wonder where the little boy was and how the rag got so muddy? Does anyone here know how such a thing could happen? [*Let them answer.*] I think you are right. But I wonder why he did not tell me that he was playing in the mud. Can you guess why? [*Let them answer.*] It could be that he was afraid, but it is also a possibility that he was ashamed.

When we are ashamed of what we do we try not to think about it. St. Paul said that Christians do not have to think about the way that they used to be because when we love Christ and become his followers then we are forgiven for all of the things that we used to do and we are living a new life. We hide the muddy rag because we are ashamed of what our shoes looked like when we were told not to play in the mud. Our muddy shoes are a sign that we did not obey. The rag could take the mud off the shoes, but the mud on the rag had to be hidden.

That is the way that all of us feel about things we are ashamed of doing. When we look down at the muddy rag we feel bad but when we see the clean shoes without the mud on them we feel good again. That's the way a Christian should feel. He is very happy about being clean, and being friends with Jesus Christ, but he is ashamed of the kinds of things that he did before he knew Jesus. When Jesus comes into your heart he makes you feel like a pair of clean shoes, but when you think of how you used to be before you knew about Jesus then you think of hiding all the bad things that made you feel ashamed. Just remember how good it is to be a Christian and to feel clean all over. Will you do that? Good.

SHARING YOUR BLOOD

*Romans 8:12-17, vs. 17: And since we are his children,
we will share his treasures — for all God gives to his
Son Jesus is now ours, too. But if we are to share his
glory, we must also share his suffering.*

*Object: Some kind of a set-up for a blood transfusion. If
nothing else there should be a syringe.*

Good morning, boys and girls. How many of you
have ever heard of a blood transfusion? Do you know
what it means to have your blood transfused? [*Let them
answer.*] That's right, it means that one person shares
his blood with another person who has real need of it.
Many times the doctor orders blood for someone after
he has been operated on, or if he has a certain kind of
illness. Without blood, the right kind of blood, people
would have terrible problems, and some would die.

When you give blood the hospital fixes you up with
a system that looks something like this. [*Show them
your set-up if you have one available.*] The nurse puts a
needle in your arm and you lie on a cot while they take
your blood out of you and transfer it to a plastic sack or,
if it is an emergency, right into the person who needs it.
It doesn't hurt, but it is not a pleasant thing to do. If
someone asked you if you wanted to give a pint of
blood or go to the movie, you would tell him that you
wanted to go to the movie. There are a lot of things that
you would rather do than give blood, but giving blood
is necessary if other people are going to live. You never
know when you are going to need someone else's
blood.

While giving blood is not easy, watching someone
get better because of it is super. It is a wonderful
feeling to watch someone get well and live happily for
many years because of the blood that you gave. I
would like to compare this to being a Christian. It is not

always easy to be a Christian. A Christian lives a certain way and does certain things. He does not do certain other things that some people who are not Christian think that they can do. Of course, God's law is for everybody, but being a Christian means that you know about God's love and his law. That is why you must do some things and not do others. Being a Christian means sharing your love and the things that you have with others. It can be a real hard job being a Christian. But then you must remember that there are the really good things that God is sharing, and will always share, with all who obey him and trust in him.

If you want to share the glory of God then you must also share the hardship of being a Christian. It is just like sharing your blood. You may not like to lie on a table and have your blood taken out of you, but it is all worth it when you see how happy and healthy you have made someone else.

"CLOSE COVER BEFORE STRIKING"

1 Corinthians 10:1-13, vs. 11: All these things happened to them as examples — as object lessons to us — to warn us against doing the same things; they were written down so that we could read about them and learn from them in these last days as the world nears its end.

Object: Some matches, some fingers bandaged that appear to have been burned and a match cover that says "Close cover before striking."

Good morning, boys and girls. Has anyone ever told you something and then said that he is telling it to you for your own good? [*Let them answer.*] I want to show you something. I wish I had listened to someone warn me so that this wouldn't have happened. [*Hold up your bandaged fingers.*] What do you think happened to me? Can you guess what I did that I shouldn't have done? [*Let them answer.*] If you think that I burned my fingers playing with matches you are right. Has anyone here burned his fingers with a match? It really hurts, and I wish I had read the match cover before I struck the match. Do you know what it says on the cover? It says that you should close the cover before you strike a match. I didn't and guess what happened? All of the matches caught fire and the fire burned my fingers. If I had read the cover and closed it first this would have never happened.

This is just an example of something else that I want to tell you about so that you will better understand the ways of God. People are always asking me about things in the Bible that happened to people. They wonder why God let people write about the bad things that happened to people who were supposed to be followers of God. The reason the men wrote about them is because they really happened. God wants us to know that when we do not follow what he teaches, we are sure to have trouble. But there is another reason and that is the one that I wanted to show you today.

I told you about the matches so that you will not make the same mistake. You should never play with matches for that is very dangerous. But if you have to use a match then you should know the right way and the wrong way so that you will not be hurt. God tells us about the bad things that happen to people who do not follow his teachings so that we will know the difference between right and wrong and always try to do the right thing. The Bible teaches us by example and if we are smart we will listen and learn what is right and what is wrong. I hope that none of you will ever burn your fingers because you forgot to read the instructions on the cover of the matches. And I hope that all of you will follow the teachings of God.

YOU'RE PART OF A JIGSAW PUZZLE

1 Corinthians 12:27-31a, vs. 27: *Now here is what I am trying to say: All of you together are the one body of Christ and each one of you is a separate and necessary part of it.*

Object: *A jigsaw puzzle.*

Good morning, boys and girls. How important are you? [*Let them answer.*] You may not feel very important since you don't have a job or make lots of money, but I want to tell you that I think you are very important, and so does Jesus. Let me show you what I mean.

A long time ago St. Paul wrote a letter to the people in the town of Corinth. He told them about their importance in the church. Not everybody felt very important, so he explained it to them this way. He said they were just like different parts of the body. Some of them were like fingers and others like arms and legs. There were a few who were like eyes and some like ears. He said that they were all important. Well, I guess Paul knew what people would think so he went even further. To make a whole body you need all of the parts, and that means the little finger is as important to the whole body as is the thumb.

Here is another way to help you understand. How many of you work puzzles? Everybody likes a puzzle. A puzzle has a lot of parts and you have to work hard to put them all together. If one piece is missing you will search and search until you find it. [*Show the puzzle with one piece missing and then two and then three.*] With each missing piece the puzzle is less and less complete. You need all of the pieces to make the puzzle whole. [*Put the pieces back until you have the whole puzzle.*]

That's the way it is with God's Church. You may think that the only person God needs is the pastor. You are wrong. Maybe the organist and the choir director. You are still wrong. The ushers, the choir and the Sunday Church School teachers. You are still wrong. God says that if his Church is going to be whole he needs every one of us because there is something important for every boy and girl and mother and father to do. It is just like a body or a puzzle with something missing. You don't know how important a finger is until you don't have one of them, or you don't know how important each piece of the puzzle is until you miss one of them. They are important, and so are you to God. Remember how much God is counting on you to do your job, and then you will know what a very important person you are in this world.

PASS IT ON!

1 Corinthians 15:1-10, vs. 3: I passed on to you right from the first what had been told me, that Christ died for our sins just as the Scriptures said he would.

Object: A baton or stick used in a relay race.

Good morning, boys and girls. How many of you have ever run a race? Every one of you has run a race, but how many of you have run a relay race? Does anyone know what the word "relay" means. [*Let them answer.*] A relay race is a race in which one person runs part of the race and then tags someone or passes something to him to finish the race. Sometimes a baton is passed from one to another. [*Show them the baton.*]

You can have a relay race with three, four or five people on a team. The important thing is that whenever one person starts to run he must carry the baton. You can't run without the baton, so it is important that you have it when you run, and it is important that you give the baton to the person who is going to run after you.

St. Paul had something to pass on and he talked about it when he wrote to the people in Corinth. Paul told the people that he was going to pass on to them something that he had received. For Paul, it wasn't a baton, but instead it was a message. Now it was just as important to Paul that he pass on to the people the exact same thing that he received as it is to a runner to pass on the same baton that he received when he started the race. It was important that Paul told the great truth he had received from God. He told the Corinthians that Jesus died for everyone's sins, just as the Scriptures said that he would even before he was born.

This is not a truth that Paul just discovered while he was wandering around some town. This isn't something that Paul figured out from talking to a friend, or from reading a book. Paul had the truth given to him by God. It was such a big idea, and such a wonderful idea, that Paul knew he had to pass it on to others like the people in Corinth. Just think, when Jesus died he did it so that we could be forgiven for all of our sins and be ready to live with God in heaven forever.

I want you to know that when Paul passed that great truth on to the people of Corinth they didn't let it stop there. They passed it on to others. That's the way it still happens today. When we hear the truth, we listen, and then pass it on. Let's see if we can do it. Let's say it together: JESUS DIED FOR OUR SINS. Now pass it on. [Let them say it.] You can tell everyone you know the good news, and this will make all of the saints in heaven, like St. Paul, very happy.

AN IMPORTANT PROMISE

Galatians 3:16-22, vs. 17: Here's what I am trying to say: God's promise to save through faith — and God wrote this promise down and signed it — could not be cancelled or changed four hundred and thirty years later when God gave the Ten Commandments.

Object: A note or house mortgage.

Good morning, boys and girls. Is there anyone here who made a promise this week? What kind of a promise was it? [*Let them answer.*] Promises are wonderful words because they are words of trust between two or more people. When you made a promise last week it made you feel good because it made you closer to someone you like.

Sometimes when we make promises that are really important we do something different than we do at other times. If it is very important we write down the promise and sign it with our names. I brought with me today an important promise like the kind I just spoke about. We call this a mortgage. When people buy houses, they sign a paper like this, which is a promise between the buyers and the bank. The bank promises to lend the people the money and the people agree to pay back the loan with some money each month. A promise like that is so important that we must sign our names and the bank must have somebody sign for it, too. Important promises have signed names on them.

God makes promises, and he puts his name under the promise so that we know how important he considers each promise he makes with us. This did not begin yesterday or last year. God has always put his name behind every promise that he makes. A long time ago God made a promise to Abraham and to all of the sons and grandsons of Abraham, and then he gave a sign to show that he meant what he promised. He didn't write it with a pen and ink, but God showed Abraham that he was behind his promise.

St. Paul remembered the story about God and Abraham when he was talking to some new church members and he told it to them. "Now," St. Paul said, "God didn't break his promises to the children and grandchildren of Abraham when he gave them the Ten Commandments." Just because God tells you something new doesn't mean that God breaks his old promises. That's the way God is. When he makes a promise he keeps it.

It's the same way with God and with us today. When Jesus promised that he would die for our sins, he meant it. It may seem like an old promise since Jesus died almost 2,000 years ago, but it is still true today. The next time you hear about people making promises about some important things like houses, I want you to remember about the promises of God and how God keeps his promises forever. Will you do that? I hope so.

SHARING

Galatians 5:25-6:10, vs. 2: Share each other's troubles and problems, and so obey our Lord's command.

Object: Cans or books too heavy for one person to carry.

Good morning, boys and girls. Today we are going to try an experiment with some volunteers. Is there anyone who would like to volunteer? I need two people to help me. [*Select two children.*]

I have brought with me some cans like those your mother buys in the grocery. I need to move these cans to the back of the church. What I am going to do is load you up with as many cans as you can carry so that we will have to make as **few** trips as possible. [*Load up one of the volunteers with all of the cans. If necessary have the same volunteer make two trips. The other volunteer should walk beside the one carrying the cans, but he should not be given any to carry.*] Now, you know that we must get the cans to the back of the church. Your friend will walk with you so that if you drop one he can pick it up and give it back to you. Let's see how long it takes you to get to the back of the church. [*Let them walk. Have the same one bring them back if you like.*]

That wasn't too bad, was it? I thought that both of our volunteers did a good job, didn't you? Is there anything wrong? Do you think I should have done something different? [*Let them answer.*] You think that I wasn't fair, and they should have shared the work. Do you think it would have been better and easier if they had both carried some? Why should both volunteers have to work hard if it is possible for only one person to work and the other take it easy? [*Let them answer.*] You think that it would be better if they shared the work.

I'm glad you feel that way. St. Paul felt the same way about Christians and living. He told the Christians in Galatia that they should share each others' problems and worries because that is the way Jesus wanted it. When we share a worry or trouble, it means that most of the time our trouble is only half as much. Christians love to help each other and they look for ways to do it. If your friend has a hard job that looks like it will take all day, then think how happy you will make him if you help. Then the job will only take half a day and you can play the rest of the time.

Helping each other with problems is the Christian way to do things. I hope you will remember to volunteer the next time your friend needs help. Okay? Okay!

POLISH WITH LOVE

2 Corinthians 3:4-9, vs. 9: If the plan that leads to doom was glorious, how much more glorious is the plan that makes man right with God.

Object: Difference between water and furniture polish to make something shine; one fades, the other stays shiny.

Good morning, boys and girls. Today we are going to show you the difference between the plan of the Old Testament and the plan in the New Testament. I have brought this dirty wooden chair up front where you can see it well. Now, if you wanted to shine this chair so that it looked beautiful again, you would have two choices. First of all, I am going to take this rag and a pan of clean water and see how lovely I can make the chair look. Now we will watch the chair closely as it drys. Can you see some of the water shine wearing off? It doesn't look as nice when it drys as it did when it was wet. Water shine doesn't last.

Now I am going to use some furniture polish on the same dusty chair. We will use the same kind of rag and work on part of the chair. Let's watch it just as we did the water part. Do you see any difference? [*Let them answer.*] It isn't fading, is it? The polish is working and it remains where the water shine faded away.

This is what Paul said is the difference between the way of law in the Old Testament and the way of love in the New Testament. When you first see the law, it looks good, it sounds good, and it feels good. But in time it fades away. No one finds God by trying to keep the law. The law tells us what we are doing that is wrong, but it cannot make us do what is right. The law fades. Now the furniture polish is the love in the New Testament and it remains. It is not only bright when it is being used, but it stays bright. That's the way love is.

God is love and God is forever. People find God with love. Love not only teaches us what is right, but we like what we learn in love.

That's the difference. The law fades, but love stays. A lot of people find out what is wrong with what they think and do when they learn the law. But when people learn in love, they not only learn what is wrong but what to do that is right.

The next time you try to polish a chair, remember what you are going to use if you have a choice between water and polish. Use the polish and it will give it a long and lasting shine. Use love with your friends and you will have long friendships. They will not fade, but will last forever. And so will your love for God.

LINES THAT GUIDE YOU

Galatians 5:16-24, vs. 18: When you are guided by the Holy Spirit you need no longer force yourself to obey Jewish laws.

Object: Some lined and some unlined paper and a pen.

Good morning, boys and girls. Today we want to talk about God in a way we don't very often. How many of you have heard about the Holy Spirit? Almost all of you, but I wonder what you think the Holy Spirit does? [*Let them answer.*] Those are some very interesting answers.

I would like to show you something that will help you to understand what the Holy Spirit does for you. I brought two kinds of paper with me for you to see. Can you tell the difference between the two pieces of paper? [*Show them both pieces.*] That's right, one piece has lines on it and the other doesn't. When we first learn how to write we need paper with lines so that our words are in order and make sense. Let me show you what I mean. [*Write some words being very careful to use the lines.*] The lines are guides when we are learning to write. Have you ever noticed what it looks like when we don't have the lines? [*Let one of the children write on the piece of paper without lines.*] Do you notice the difference? The lines are guides, and this is one of the things that reminds us of the Holy Spirit.

The Holy Spirit is a guide for people just as lines are for words. The Holy Spirit is God helping us to stay true to the teachings of Jesus and the love of God. The Holy Spirit reminds us how to help a neighbor who is sick or lonely. The Holy Spirit guides us to tell the truth even when we would like to say something else. The Holy Spirit guides us to share some of our money with a man who doesn't have any. The Holy Spirit guides us to be members of Christ's church and to worship.

Without the Holy Spirit and his guidance we would be like a person learning to write without lines. Lines are important to writers, and the Holy Spirit is necessary to all Christians. The next time you see a piece of paper you should check to see if it has lines or not. Either way, you will remember that the Holy Spirit is the guide of our lives.

GOD'S LOVE IS LIKE A ROOT

Ephesians 3:13-21, vs. 17: And I pray that Christ will be more and more at home in your hearts, living within you as you trust in him. May your roots go down deep into the soil of God's marvelous love.

Object: Some soil and a plant with roots.

Good morning, boys and girls. Today we are going to look at something that is familiar to us, yet it is still a mystery. I brought some plants that grow in our gardens during the summer and some that we grow in our homes during the winter. Plants are special to God's creation and they work in many ways. What does a plant need to make it grow? [*Let them answer.*] Yes, it does need sunshine and it does need rain, but what else does a plant need if it is to make a flower or a vegetable? That's right, it needs soil, or the good earth.

I brought along some soil from my yard so that we could see some of the mystery of God's ways. If I took you and planted you in the soil, do you think that you would grow? What if I took a fish and put it in the ground. Would it grow? Of course not. People, fish and animals do not grow in the ground. A worm does not grow in the ground as if it was planted. But plants do grow in the ground. Part of the plant grows under the ground and part of it grows above the ground. Do you know what we call the part of the plant under the ground? That's right, we call that part the roots. Strong roots make a strong plant. You can't have weak roots and strong plants. The roots are important, the stem is important, but so is the ground that the plant is living in. Have you ever tried to pull out a plant that has roots that go deep into the ground? That is almost impossible.

St. Paul knew something about plants and roots, but he also knew a lot about the ground. Paul compared people and plants with God and the ground. Paul said that people should let their feelings about God grow deep into God's love. He said it in a little different way. He said that people should let their roots grow deep into the soil of God's love. In other words, Paul said that what we need is God's love, just as a plant's roots need good soil. If you go all the way and trust in God's love, then you will be as hard to pull out as a plant that lets its roots grow deep into the ground. People who trust and love God that much are happy and full of love since they receive so much love from God. With roots like this below the ground, you can imagine how strong you will look above the ground.

It was a pretty good way for Paul to tell us about our need for the love of God. The next time you see some roots on a plant, think about how much they want to get into the soil and then you will think about all the love that God has waiting for you.

ALLOWING FOR MISTAKES

Ephesians 4:1-6, vs. 2: Be humble and gentle. Be patient with each other, making allowance for each other's faults because of your love.

Object: A typewriter and eraser.

Good morning, boys and girls. How many of you made a mistake this week? Did anyone here do something that he would consider a mistake and wishes that he had not done it? [*Let them answer.*] Tell me about some of your mistakes. [*Let them give you a few examples of what they felt they did wrong.*] After you made the mistake, did you do anything about it? I want to know if you corrected your mistake. I think that one of the biggest mistakes that people make is the way we treat each other. We do a lot of things that hurt ourselves and we generally take care of them; but what do we do when we hurt each other?

Most machines make room for errors. Let me show you what I mean. I brought along my typewriter because I make more mistakes on this than anything else I use. When I am typing a letter or a sermon I make a lot of mistakes and I must correct them or no one else will be able to read what I write. The typewriter lets me correct my mistakes and goes to a lot of trouble so that I can do this. Let me show you what I mean. If I misspell a word I can stop the machine and go back to where I made the mistake and erase it, then type in the new letter and go on. If I skip a word or a letter I can back the machine up as many spaces as I want to until I find the place that I skipped and then correct it. If I did not judge correctly how long a word was going to be and I went past the place the machine stops, I press the margin release and type on. My typewriter allows me to correct the mistakes I make.

St. Paul listened to God and found out that it was just as important for us to allow other people to make mistakes as it was for God to allow us to make mistakes. We need to use some of our love to allow other people to make mistakes and not get angry with them over the mistakes that they make. That means that we are not only forgiving but it also means that we know that everyone is not perfect. If you know this and make up your mind that you are not going to be angry every time someone does something wrong, then you are going to have a lot of friends and you are also going to be a better Christian. Christians love their friends not because of all the things they do that are right, but because they are children of God who want to be loved just as we want to be loved.

A typewriter knows that there are going to be mistakes and it allows for them. So must Christians allow for the mistakes that other people make.

IT'S GUARANTEED!

1 Corinthians 1:4-9, vs. 8: And he guarantees right up to the end that you will be counted free from all sin and guilt on that day when he returns.

Object: Some form of a guarantee cut from a newspaper or magazine.

Good morning, boys and girls. How many of you have ever heard the saying, "This is guaranteed or your money back"? Do you know what that means? [*Let them answer.*] That's right. It means that whatever you buy that has a guarantee will do what it is supposed to do or you can get all your money back. I know a lot of people who will buy only certain kinds of clothes because they know that the clothes are guaranteed. There are a lot of things which are guaranteed, and when you buy these things you need never worry. Most of the time the thing that you buy with a guarantee works just as the people who sold it to you said it would. But, if for some reason there is something wrong with it, then they will always give you your money back no matter how long you have used it or worn it. That is a guarantee.

There is another guarantee that I want to talk about this morning that is just as good as any that you have ever heard of or seen. There is the guarantee that when Jesus comes back to earth he will accept you as part of his group of believers and members of God's world forever. For everyone who believes today and tomorrow have all of the good things that Jesus gives to us in this life; but we also will have all of the good things in the life to come. That is guaranteed. Jesus promised it and we know that his guarantee is true. We don't have to wait until the new world to be happy, to have love, to be without fear. We can have those things today when we believe in Jesus. But I want to tell you that the guarantee is that they will not stop here but will go on and on forever.

Some people wonder if God can keep such wonderful promises. People wonder if heaven can be such a good place for just believing that Jesus is the Son of God. The answer to that question is: don't wait until then to find out. If you want to see if God's guarantee is good, then try him out now. See if what he promises you comes true today. That is the guarantee of God. He will not only take care of you today but he will also take care of you in heaven. The other way is true also. God does not only guarantee you that you will find happiness in heaven, but he guarantees it to all of his believers here on earth. The next time that you hear someone make you a guarantee about something that you want to buy, I want you to think about the guarantee that God makes to all believers.

A PRIZE FOR EVERYONE — ALMOST

Romans 3:21-28, vs. 23: Yes, all have sinned; and fall short of God's glorious ideal.

Object: Some string and some lifesavers or pieces of candy.

Good morning, boys and girls. How many of you like contests? Almost all boys and girls like to see who is the best at what they are doing. The only thing is that we already know who is the best in the contest that I am going to have you do today. The olympic champion has jumped with a running start 27 feet and so many inches. I have measured this out in the aisle of our church and I am going to give every child here a chance to see if he can set a new world's record. It isn't going to be easy, but then a world's record is something that does not happen to every person. Also, I want to tell you that everyone who breaks the world record is going to get a prize of one lifesaver. Now if you will all line up at the back of the church and jump when you reach this line [*first piece of string*] and see if you can jump as far as this line [*the second piece of string.*] Remember, we already know what the best is, so you must do at least this well if you want a prize. [*Proceed to let them each take their turn at jumping.*]

Isn't that a disappointment? Not one of you could beat the world's record. You tried to beat that which was perfect, and you could not make it. However, I want you to know that since you tried and you finished the contest I am going to give each of you a prize anyway. I want you to know that all of you failed to set a record, but you are still getting the prize. I also want you to know that I am giving a prize not only to the one who jumped the farthest or the highest, but to everyone who took part in the contest.

There is a reason why I am doing this. I want you to understand something about God. As you and I know there are certain things about God that none of us can ever have. God is perfect. He has perfect love and he has perfect law. God is perfection. God is the world record holder in anything that is important. He is perfectly honest, perfectly intelligent, perfect in love, perfect in forgiveness and so forth. God is perfect. He tells us what is perfect and asks us to try to be perfect in our love and honesty and so forth. None of us is. All of us are short when we measure and see how far we have gone and how far it is to being perfect like God.

But God doesn't fail us for that. God still gives us his love and life even though we have fallen short. The prize will be ours because we tried, even though we failed. It is important that we try. The next time you run a race or jump, you can remember the way that God does it and how he gives prizes to losers. We are all losers when we compare ourselves to God, but we are all winners when we know that God gives the prize to all who stay in his contest called life, and believe that he is God.

GOD'S SPECIAL FAMILY

Revelation 7:2-17, vs. 3: "Wait! Don't do anything yet — hurt neither earth nor sea nor trees — until we have placed the Seal of God upon the foreheads of his servants."

Object: A coat of arms [Can be borrowed from any gift shop]

Good morning, boys and girls. Today we want to talk about belonging, and how you can tell how some people belong and others don't. I have with me something that tells me about belonging. [*Hold up the coat of arms.*] Have you ever seen one of these? [*Let them answer.*] This is called a Coat of Arms. A long time ago families would design a coat of arms and put their family name on it, and every member of that family would use it. Every home had a coat of arms hanging somewhere in the house. They also used the design on their armor, their flag and just about everything they could to tell people who they were, and to whom they belonged. All people want to belong to someone, and they also want someone to belong to them. Some people still have a coat of arms in their homes today.

God knows that everyone wants to belong and that is why he calls those who believe in him his family. Christians have always felt that they should have a sign of belonging to God. The writer of the book of Revelation said that the Christians who died for Christ had a special marking which all other Christians would recognize. Our baptism is a sign of belonging to God. All Christians are baptized as a sign of being a member of God's family.

The next time that you see one of these Coats of Arms you will think about belonging to a family. That kind of thinking will also remind you that you belong to a larger family, some who have died for Jesus, and the name of that family is Christian. The Christian family is the family of God.

GOD GIVES YOU

Ephesians 6:10-17, vs. 13: So use every piece of God's armor to resist the enemy whenever he attacks, and when it is all over, you will still be standing up.

Object: A sandwich: mustard, lettuce, bread, meat, etc.

Good morning, boys and girls. How many of you like to eat? Oh, that's good. How many like to eat sandwiches? Oh, that's really good. My favorite kind of food is a sandwich. What is a sandwich? [*Let them answer.*] A sandwich is bread, meat, mustard, lettuce, pickles and other good things. In other words, a sandwich is made up of many things. The more things that I can put between two pieces of bread, the better I like it.

That's the way that God feels about you and the devil. God says that he wants us to use all of the things that he has given us so we can defeat the Devil. God gave us a lot of different things. He gave us love, patience, prayer, kindness, mercy, faith and much more so that we would never be afraid when the Devil attacks us. Using all of the things that God gives us keeps the Devil far away and afraid, because he knows that you have God's power on your side and God's power is like a sandwich. It has love on one side and faith on the other, and in between it has all of these other things I have mentioned.

So the next time that you see a sandwich and it has lots of good things in between the two pieces of bread, you can think about the way that God prepares you to fight against the Devil. He gives you peace, prayer and kindness and many other things, including love on one end and faith on the other. No wonder the Devil is afraid of God and his people when they are that well prepared. How many of you will use the things that God has given you, so that you will be prepared? That's wonderful!

FINISHED JELL-O

Philippians 1:3-11, vs. 6: And I am sure that God who began the good work within you will keep right on helping you grow in his grace until his task within you is finally finished on that day when Jesus Christ returns.

Object: Jell-O [Some in liquid state, some in solid state]

Good morning, boys and girls. How many of you got off to a good beginning this morning? Oh, that's good. How many of you will have a good ending tonight? Lots of people have good beginnings, but only a few have good endings. Let me show you what I mean.

I have with me this morning one of your favorite foods. It's called jello. How many of you like jello? Almost everybody. When your mom makes jello it looks like this in the beginning. [*Show liquid jello.*] How many of you like your jello this way? Hmmm, not many of you. When the jello is watery, it isn't finished. It is a good beginning, but what must you do to make sure that it has a good ending? That's right, you must put it in the refrigerator and let it set till it gets like this. [*Show finished jello.*] This jello had both a good beginning and a good ending.

The reason that I showed you the two kinds of jello is that God is interested in working with you not only when you are children, or when you begin your Christian lives, but God wants to work with you always. God does not start something without finishing it, and he promises that he will work with you as long as you live in this world, and also when you live with him in heaven. God is not a quitter. He finishes everything he starts. What he teaches, he also does, and his love and work with you is eternal.

The next time that you sit down to eat a dish of jello, I want you to remember that God is working with you now just as he worked with you before and just as he will work with you tomorrow. Whatever God begins he also finishes. Do you all understand that? Good. See you all next week.